Alice G Howard

Ours

Alice G Howard

Ours

ISBN/EAN: 9783744651981

Printed in Europe, USA, Canada, Australia, Japan

Cover: Foto ©Thomas Meinert / pixelio.de

More available books at **www.hansebooks.com**

OURS

BY

ALICE G. HOWARD

.

―――

"Not mine and thine,
But ours, for ours is thine and mine."

—LONGFELLOW.

―――

SAN FRANCISCO

C. A. MURDOCK & CO.

1890

NOT FOR ITS PERFECTION, BUT FOR THE
LOVE I BEAR THEE.

"

FOR THE MASTER.

Lord, from Thy store of bread give me a crumb :
May I so use it that it may become
Food for my soul, and to the needy light :
Drink to the thirsty, to the blind ones sight.
From Thine own hand, O Lord, give it to me ;
Keep me so near that Thy sweet face I'll see ;
Breathe into it a wondrous power of love,
For Thine own glory, Lord, here as above.

Master, my basket bring I unto Thee ;
Emptied of self, in deep humility,
No laurel crown entreat I at Thy hand,
Just daily strength to follow Thy command :
Fill it, dear Lord, with little words and deeds ;
(Not yet the "waving palms") God's tiny seeds :
Hide in each one the germ of life divine ;
Naught shall then "void return"—The Word is Thine.

Steep mountain sides and cliffs I cannot scale ;
Even in sunny fields my footsteps fail.
Here in the valley, Lord, I sit and try
To bring refreshment to the passers-by.
Lord, may the sweeping winds that round me blow,
Cause Thy dear cherished seeds to farther go ;
Sown on the breeze, the fruit I cannot see ;
O garner, Lord ! — I sow them all for Thee.

LIKE A WHITE ROSE.

I hold thee in my hands, thou rose celestial,
    And search thy depths for trace of mark or stain.
I part thy waxy leaves with touch relentless,
    And e'en to break thee I do not disdain.
The more I bruise thee, sweeter comes thy perfume :
    Thy heart is filled with rays of morning light.
The closer sight reveals the greater beauty :
    No secret blemish ; naught to dwarf or blight.

Lord, who didst make the rose in its perfection,
    Cast on my heart Thy penetrating gaze.
Spare not one blot, however small or hidden ;
    My soul unto Thy spotless standard raise.
Bruise, if Thou wilt, my lips shall sing Thy praises,
    For only good can come from Thy dear hand.
My inner life shall store bright rays of gladness
    To drop like petals, at Thy loved command.

Come cloud or sunshine, may I grow and blossom,
    Broadening out, though many times cut down.
I would not seek to gain the world's approval,
    But watch Thy face lest I should make Thee frown.
I am so weak, O Father, do Thou for me ;
    The evening tarries ; slow the coming morn.
In Thee is strength ; I will not fear the breezes
    That but perfect the rose, without a thorn.

COME UNTO ME.

"Come unto Me." Soft falls the tender pleading;
  Come, weary souls, and I will give you rest.
Why will ye labor, worn and heavy laden?
  Sure are My wages, and My service blest.
My yoke is easy, and light is My burden;
  My heart is lowly, and My soul is love.
I am the Way unto the many mansions;
  Come, follow me, I lead to God above.

Come, I would gather, as the hen her chickens,
  Each struggling frame within My loving arms.
Who looks to Me for strength and firm protection,
  Earth may assail, but nothing ever harms.
I am the Bread for souls athirst and hungry,
  Refuge and help in ev'ry time of need.
I am the Light; they shall not walk in darkness
  Who seek My face and My commandments heed.

Come and inherit all My bright possessions,
  Freedom from sin, and peace forever more.
Thou shalt not see by *faith* the Lord of glory,
  But *face to face* the King whom saints adore.
"Come unto Me"; let them that hear repeat it;
  Death cannot chain; My power is divine.
Who trusts in Me shall reach the gates eternal,
  And enter in, for all who come are Mine.

TO A TRUE FRIEND.

When I sit beside the river,
  In the land of peace and rest;
When life's trials all are over,
  And my soul is with the blest —
Do you think I will forget you,
  Though I seem so far away?
Do you think I will not love you
  As I love you, dear, to-day?
Would I really be myself, dear,
  If my heart should prove untrue!
Could I be supremely happy,
  And not give one thought to you?
I shall think of one who led me
  When the way was long and drear;
I shall think of one whose courage
  Taught my own heart not to fear;
I shall tell the blessed Master
  Of the words you spoke for Him,
When my heart was heavy laden
  And my eyes with tears were dim.
I shall tell Him you were faithful
  In example and in prayer;
Then when you meet His smiling face
  You will read a welcome there.
" Bear ye one another's burdens "
  Is a sacred, sweet command,
And it brings to such as you, dear,
  A reward from God's own hand.

"THEY SHALL SEE GOD."

I walked through fields of summer verdure,
    And read the lessons written there
In tiny spires pointing heavenward,
    And lilies blooming fresh and fair:
I saw God's face in smiling blossoms,
    I read His strength in spreading trees,
I felt within my soul the blessing
    That God's own hand was in the breeze.

It touched my cheek in tender pity,
    It kissed my brow with words of love:
It whispered to my heart that comfort
    Which cometh only from above.
The dew was still upon the flowers,
    The sun just peeping o'er the hill,
I prayed, "O God, whose grace aboundeth,
    With warmth and peace my spirit fill.

"Keep me so pure, that as I journey
    With eager steps along life's way,
I may behold Thee, close beside me,
    And years seem but a gladsome day.
But should I leave the fresh green pastures,
    And reach a hard and barren land,
O Father, clasp me all the closer,
    And let me cling to Thy strong hand.

9

" Make Thou my lips to sing Thy praises,
  My face to beam with holy light;
A guide to those who would find Jesus,
  The weary pilgrims of the night.
Lord, when my feet have reached the summit,
  And stand before the jasper throne,
May I not meet Thee empty-handed,
  Nor enter Heaven's gates alone."

THE NIGHT LISTENS.

Night drew her sable mantle o'er her starlit face,
  And bent her head each whispered sound to hear :
Above her throbbing heart her snowy hands firm
    clasped,
  Her lips compressed, restraining inward fear.
Will man forget his Maker when the shadows fall?
  Can one forget who gives the weary rest?
She opened wide the book suspended from her arm,
  And crooned in slumber notes — "Peace to the
    blest" —
As if her words awakened sacred thoughts below,
  An incense sweet filled all the silent air.
In rolling puffs, in clouds, in winding columns strong,
  Arose, like smoke from fire, man's earnest prayer.

O Night! thou wakeful nurse, brooding thy children
    dear,
  Would that thy loving hand need not record
And seal with bitter tears wrung from thy watchful
    eyes,
  That *some* men slept, nor even *thought* of God.

EVENTIDE.

In the evening time, when sounds are still,
And love for Thee my hungry heart doth fill,
Soft and low, like a mother's lullaby,
I hear Thy voice from out the vaulted sky.
The heavens part, a form divinely fair,
Floats through the stillness, filling all the air
With words so sweet, so comforting to me,
I kneel in silence, knowing, Lord, 't is Thee.

Thy spirit dwelling in the soul of man,
Joins earth to Heaven by a single span.
With curtains drawn upon our earthly gaze,
Our hearts illumined by Thy holy rays,
We see Thee, Lord, as standing face to face,
And on Thy hands our graven names can trace.
Is it not Heaven, O our God divine,
To meet with Thee and feel that we are Thine?

A quiet hour, a list'ning heart, Thy voice,
Inspire me, Lord, to seek and make my choice.
Obedience prompt for Thy commands when heard;
A soul at rest to catch the faintest word.
Be Thou my light, my guidance, my control;
Accept, O Lord, my *body* and my *soul:*
And thus, the " earthen vessel " glorified,
Both shall be Thine when comes the eventide.

EVENTIDE.

In the evening time, when sounds are still,
And love for Thee my hungry heart doth fill,
Soft and low, like a mother's lullaby,
I hear Thy voice from out the vaulted sky.
The heavens part, a form divinely fair,
Floats through the stillness, filling all the air
With words so sweet, so comforting to me,
I kneel in silence, knowing, Lord, 't is Thee.

Thy spirit dwelling in the soul of man,
Joins earth to Heaven by a single span.
With curtains drawn upon our earthly gaze,
Our hearts illumined by Thy holy rays,
We see Thee, Lord, as standing face to face,
And on Thy hands our graven names can trace.
Is it not Heaven, O our God divine,
To meet with Thee and feel that we are Thine?

A quiet hour, a list'ning heart, Thy voice,
Inspire me, Lord, to seek and make my choice.
Obedience prompt for Thy commands when heard;
A soul at rest to catch the faintest word.
Be Thou my light, my guidance, my control;
Accept, O Lord, my *body* and my *soul:*
And thus, the " earthen vessel " glorified,
Both shall be Thine when comes the eventide.

LIFE BEYOND.

" He that believeth on the Lord hath everlasting life."

Do not hush the little pattering feet,
    Or merry voices sounding on the stair;
O do not say, through quickly falling tears,
    When I am gone, behold your mother there;
But pointing heavenward, with hands outstretched,
    Tell of the glory of that land beyond,
Where one they loved has sought the mercy-seat
    Of Him above all earthly friends most fond.

Tell them there is no death to those who love,
    But one eternal, everlasting day;
With naught of sickness, sorrow, or of grief,
    For God the Father casteth all away.
Tell them of rivers flowing through that land,
    Beside whose banks the tree of life doth grow,
Laden with fruit of many different kinds,
    And leaves which heal the Nations' ev'ry woe.

Tell them that God doth there reveal His face
    Unto His children kneeling at His feet;
He speaks to them in words of tender love,
    And hath a smile, His weakest child to greet.
O mansions fair, within the house of God,
    Thou land of rest for which the pilgrim cries,
The soul shall *live* which enters in thy gates,
    Asleep in Christ, the Christian *never dies.*

HIS LAMBS.

"Of such is the Kingdom of Heaven."

Sweet little Linda sits out in the sun,
With dainty fingers, stringing one by one
    A chain of beads.
I watch the glimmer of her golden hair,
I note her cheeks with witching dimples fair,
    And wonder.

O fairy maid, so free from care or fears,
No anxious thought for all the coming years,
    Sweetly trusting;
What lessons bring you to our time-worn hearts?
What is the hope your innocence imparts?
    I listen.

You gather sunbeams in your joyous play,
With which to frighten all our clouds away;
    Dear Comforter.
So may we glean a store of gladsome cheer,
To give to those who find life's pathway drear,
    In blessing.

Like beads upon your silken chain,
God's mercies o'er His trusting children rain
    In varied hues.

We string them, one by one, along the strand
Which binds our helplessness to God's own hand,
        Day by day.

You tie a knot, and all your work is done,
And smiling still, you sleep at set of sun
        So peacefully.
O God, when all our work is finished too,
And lovingly the knot is tied by you,
        Accept us.

BABY.

What shall I wish for thee, sweet baby dear?
A life of joy, no trace of grief or tear?
All sunshine's glimmer, without cloud or rain?
A long bright summer's day, no touch of pain?
My human heart, with judgment weak and blind,
Would crave amiss when most it would be kind.
To choose all joy would be to take from thee,
That peace which comes from setting others free
From burdens heavy, and from sorrow's blight,
And, though it grieve thee, makes thy spirit bright.
No clouds?—No rain?—The rainbow, dear, unfurls
God's loving smile, which turns our tears to pearls.
The summer ripens, and the frost makes strong.
May thy dear life be rich and pure and long:
Rich in its sweetness; and its length of days
Be one grand pæan to thy Maker's praise.
Darling, may God bless thee, is my prayer,
And close enfold thee in His loving care.

FATHER.

O hills ! majestic in your towering might,
With stony fingers pointing towards the light;
O lofty trees ! whose swaying boughs impart
A holy sense of greatness to the heart ;
I close my eyes, and bending low I cry,
Mid all this grandeur, Lord, pray what am I ?

Great is Thy power ; greater still the love
Which ruleth over all, yet from above
Speaks to the soul, in wooing accents mild,
"I am thy Father—Come and be My child."

Like babes, our steps are feeble, Lord, and slow ;
We cannot stand alone, but well we know
That round us, everlasting arms entwine,
And boundless strength and wisdom both are Thine.
Thy *children*, Father !—Words with blessing fraught ;
God grant that we may prize them as we ought.

TO-MORROW.

Yesterday we planned to-morrow's golden deeds,
    Its acts of kindness, words of loving cheer.
To-day we cry "To-morrow radiant gleams,"
    And fail to see to-morrow now is here.
We load to-day with burdens dark and heavy,
    That crush within our hearts life's gladsome song,
And look in vain to find the "silver lining"
    To clouds that make our pathway drear and long.

Alas! at times, the blackness of the present,
    Drapes e'en to-morrow with its sable pall;
And shrinking neath the weight of desolation,
    We see but death abiding over all.
O human hearts! why will ye seek to borrow
    Aught but the hours God giveth one by one?
Canst thou divide the present from the future,
    Or count thy days by rising of the sun?

To-day to-morrow is— *To-morrow, never:*
    Then catch the passing moments as they fly.
Fill ev'ry second with some hidden treasure
    To carry upward to the realms on high.
Live thou to-day—'T is death that rules to-morrow;
    The Christian's hope is everlasting life :
Time lulls this frame to rest in gentle slumber,
    And wafts the spirit far from care or strife.

JESUS ONLY.

In secret, Lord, I bend the knee in prayer;
The door is closed, no form but Thine is there.
My hands I fold; I would not raise for grace,
Aught but the nail-prints to my Maker's face.
My trembling lips refuse to form a word,
But by Thine ear each whispered thought is heard.
My eyes I close, and looking thus within,
Behold my weakness and a depth of sin.

I hear Thy voice—"Come unto Me; confess:
In Me is strength; I am thy righteousness.
Thy scarlet sins shall be as white as snow,
Thy straying feet be taught the way to go.
No human power can overcome alone,
I am the royal road unto the throne.
Come, lay thy head upon My loving breast,
Thy load is heavy but in Me is rest."

O Lord Divine, my Saviour and my friend,
I read the message which Thy love doth send
In smiling flowers, and in laughing breeze,
In songbird's twitter and in swaying trees:
I read Thy greatness in the thunder's roar,
And learn to fear Thee while I love Thee more.
Thy rod and staff both bind my soul to Thee;
Spare not one stroke that tends to purity.

My Lord, I love Thee : well Thou knowest this ;
To do Thy will I count the highest bliss.
To be like Thee, is my ambition strong ;
Purge me of dross and blot out ev'ry wrong.
Stay not Thy hand though I rebel and cry ;
My trusting heart upon the wheel doth lie.
Come weal or woe the Master holdeth me ;
So, polish, Lord, 'till Thou Thy face canst see.

LITTLE GLORIES.

There is an upward pathway, by tiny footsteps trod,
Which leads from our enfolding, into the arms of God.
Thus, day by day and hourly, the little ones take flight,
Away from nights of darkness, to everlasting light.
In notes of sweetest music, their merry voices ring :
"We are the lambs of Jesus"—the joyous song they
    sing.
Their happy faces glimmer with a celestial glow,
Reflecting Christ's own glory, like sunlight on the
    snow.
O Glory—little Glory! by whom our life was blest,
All Heaven is the brighter for this lone cradle-nest.
"Of such is God's own Kingdom," our loving Saviour
    said,
And though our arms are empty, we know thou art
    not dead.

CHRISTMAS.

When Mary bent her sweet face down,
   And pressed on baby lips a kiss,
Did shadowy cross before her loom
   To rob her of a mother's bliss?
Forgotten were her trials deep,
   Forgotten future grief and care;
The cradled Star was hers to love;
   The Babe of Bethlehem lay there.
Wise men drew near with off'rings rich,
   To crown Him infant Lord and King;
Angelic voices, from the clouds,
   Made Heaven and earth with anthems ring.
A *Christmas gift* sent down to earth,
   A *Christmas gift* for young and old;
Salvation for a sinful world,
   Salvation was the tale they told!
The tiny babe to manhood grew,
   Through years of sorrow, toil, and pain;
But at this holy Christmas time,
   We celebrate His birth again.
He came that we might be forgiven,
   And share with Him the Home above.
He gave Himself for our redemption:
   Was crucified and died for love.

Before Thy cross, with tearful eyes,
   We plead for pardon, Lord Divine.
Beside Thy cradle, "born again"
   Accept us, Lord, and make us Thine.

CONSOLATION.

The sun is sinking low, my darling,
  The stars appearing one by one :
They beam and smile like angels' faces,
  Rejoicing that the day is done.
For O, they know how hard the trials,
  The thorny pathway we have trod,
And cheer us with the fond assurance,
  That there is perfect peace with God.
Heaven is near, when we consider
  That love is there the law and rule,
The bitterness of earth's affliction,
  Is but the kindness of the school.
The Master's heart is ever tender,
  His eyes are full of loving care :
E'en when we grope in midnight darkness,
  We know His hand is hidden there.
No tear-drop falls without His notice,
  No sob but penetrates His ear.
The soul that rests in His enfolding,
  Secure in Him, hath naught to fear.
The cross we bear is spiked and heavy ;
  Shall we not glory in its thorns?
Remember Him, once bruised and broken,
  Whom now the victor's crown adorns.
Alone, forsaken in His sorrow,
  No friendly hand to clasp His own :

The only kiss a traitor's off'ring,
 No word to make affection known.
O darling, we are blessed with riches,
 The golden treasure of His love ;
No arrow strikes our human weakness,
 Which hath not pierced the Lord above.

I THANK THEE.

I thank Thee, Lord, for trials sent :
It is the twig by breezes bent,
 That firmer clasps the ground.
I thank Thee for the bitter word
That makes *Thy* voice still plainer heard,
 A tender, loving sound.

I thank Thee for the tears that wean
My soul from earth, and make it clean,
 Washed in a molten fire.
I thank Thee for Thy staff and rod,
Both mercies, in the hand of God,
 Guiding ever higher.

I thank Thee for the joy I find
In sins forgiven, cast behind
 Thy back, forever more :
I thank Thee, for in this I look
By faith, into Thy record book,
 And read my own name o'er.

I thank Thee for the light and shade
Of which this earthly life is made,
    A sacred, holy plan.
I thank Thee for the Home above,
Eternity of boundless love,
    Prepared for ransomed man.

Lord, may I ever thankful be,
Thy dear, strong arms enfolding me,
    No will but Thine to know.
Then when I meet Thee face to face,
Upon my spirit Thou canst trace
    The lessons learned below.

VIOLETS.

Dear little faces, cool and moist with rain.
Lift up your heads and kiss me once again.
Your breath so fragrant, fills my heart with rest :
Your gentle presence makes my spirit blest.
I whisper to you words of tender love ;
You nod and smile, then raise your eyes above.
Ah yes ! I know the story you would tell :
Our gracious Father doeth all things well.
He made you *little*, yet he made you *great;*
Who can compute the worth of man's estate?
One may be feeble and in body spent,
And yet fulfill the part by Heaven sent.
Good night — I kiss each tiny face once more :
I 'll not forget you on the better shore.

THINE AND MINE.

When o'er thy soul there creeps a sacred joy:
The knowledge that within thine inmost life,
Part of thy self, and spirit of thine own,
A gentle dove seeks shelter from earth's strife:
When thine own heart this truth canst not deny,
That two fond lives thus blend by grace Divine,
Forget not thou from whence the treasure comes,
But whisper gently, "Saviour, Thine and Mine."

Let her find peace within thy loving arms;
Thy breast a pillow for her weary head:
Thine eyes a gateway into realms of bliss,
Where naught but purity is ever read.
From out thy lips distill, like morning dew
O'er blushing fruit upon the clinging vine,
Bright words of praise to this fair gift of God,
Still adding softly, "Saviour, Thine and Mine."

O love is holy — Set apart for man:
The very essence of our God on high.
The prize for which the youthful ever strive,
The crown for which the aged long and cry.
Love is the inspiration of man's mind:
'T is love's great glory makes the heavens shine;
So when thou foldest to thine heart such wealth,
Say, ever humbly, "Saviour, Thine and Mine."

SUNDOWN.

If thou wert young I would not wish for thee
A life all joy, from ev'ry sorrow free,
Lest glare of sun without a drop of rain,
Bring in the end a harvesting of pain.
The path all light man shrinks from in dismay:
Unhedged by darkness many lose the way.
Unfolded plans reveal God's mighty mind:
As witnessed by the years now passed behind.
Yet rather should I say gone on before;
Recorded in God's book forever more.
My heart may crave but cannot touch the past:
The future mine—God bless thee to the last.
"What has been, may be," is a maxim true;
Incoming years may usefulness renew.
Thy cheerful face has been a beacon-light
To guide the youthful ever towards the right;
And He who died for all beheld above,
How thou didst teach the little ones to love.
"What has been, may be," I again repeat:
A faithful soldier knoweth not defeat.
A hush comes o'er me as these lines I end;
A silent longing some sweet thought to send,
Which, like the clasp of tender, loving hand,
May bear thee upward where the "Better Land"
Spreads wide its gates unto the spirit's gaze,
And lures us homeward by its golden rays.
I seem to see the dear ones gone before,
Like children waiting at the Father's door.

Their happy faces wear a watchful smile;
Soft voices echo—"Just a little while"—
Though earth enrich and lengthy be our stay,
God yet reserves a crown—a grand *Birthday*.

LOVE.

List! a plaintive song at the close of day —
It rises and falls, then dieth away,
Like the stroke of a harp by angel hand,
Or a wandering note from Fairy Land.
A calm, sweet face, with brow like riven snow,
Pink-tinted cheeks, a summer sunset glow,
Long, drooping lashes, shading dreamy eyes,
Two dainty hands, uplifted to the skies.

THE SONG.

Hear my pleading, Lord Divine,
Comfort this sad heart of mine.
Bend Thy list'ning ear to me,
Whom have I on earth but Thee?
Thou who camest from above,
Sanctifying human love,
Give me strength to bear this pain,
Help me, Lord, to smile again ;
By this silent mound of earth,
Sorrow in my heart finds birth.
Teach me, Lord, to look away,
Unto realms of endless day,

Where my Love, from trials free,
Finds sweet peace and rest with Thee.
Some glad time, when life is past,
And I come to Thee at last,
Grant, dear Father — his and mine —
That *both* souls may then be Thine.

Still lower falls the tender, pleading song,
The stars appear, as if the sacred throng,
In answer, sent forth rays of golden light,
To prove that love dispelleth darkest night.
Love is undying — God Himself is love —
'Tis shadowed here, perfected up above.
The precious clay lies in the ground to sleep,
The spirit wakes, no more to sigh or weep.

GOOD-BYE.

Good-bye—'T was planned that we should meet and
      part ;
Then let us do so with a cheerful heart.
This life is but the night time, not the day,
Not the real sunlight, just a wooing ray ;
A gleam from out the realms of endless light,
A promise that our faith shall soon be sight.
Good-bye—I kiss my finger tips to you—
Keep thy lamp trimmed, and to mankind be true.

www.ingramcontent.com/pod-product-compliance
Lightning Source LLC
Chambersburg PA
CBHW031752090426
42739CB00008B/986